CW00731760

BRANCH LINES AROUND
TIVERTON

including the Hemyock Branch

Vic Mitchell and Keith Smith

MP Middleton Press

Cover picture: Saturday rush hour at Tiverton on 4th August 1962! No. 1466 has just arrived in the bay platform on the left with the 1.22pm from Tiverton Junction, while in the distance no. 1451 waits to propel the 1.5 from Dulverton to Exeter St. Davids. No. 1471 (right) had left there at 12.50 and is ready to depart for Dulverton at 1.38. (S.P.Derek)

Back cover: Map of the lines in 1955, with the album route marked in red. (Railway Magazine)

Published February 2001
First reprint August 2013
Second reprint June 2019
Third reprint May 2020
Fourth reprint January 2022
Fifth reprint August 2022
Sixth reprint February 2024

ISBN 978 1 901706 62 8

© Middleton Press, 2001

Design   Deborah Esher
Typesetting   Barbara Mitchell

Published by
        Middleton Press
        126a Camelsdale Road
        Haslemere
        GU27 3RJ
Tel: 01730 813169
Email: info@middletonpress.co.uk
www.middletonpress.co.uk

Printed by Mapseeker Digital Ltd, Unit 15, Bridgwater Court, Oldmixon Crescent, Weston Super Mare, North Somerset, BS24 9AY.   Telephone +44 (0) 01922 458288 +44 (0) 7947107248

SECTIONS

1. Exeter to Dulverton 1-72
2. Tiverton to Tiverton Junction 73-85
3. Tiverton Junction to Hemyock 86-120

ACKNOWLEDGEMENTS

We are very grateful for the help received from so many photographers. Our thanks also go to W.R.Burton, G.Croughton, F.Hornby, N.Langridge, D.Trevor Rowe, Mr D. and Dr S.Salter, E.Youldon and our ever supportive wives.

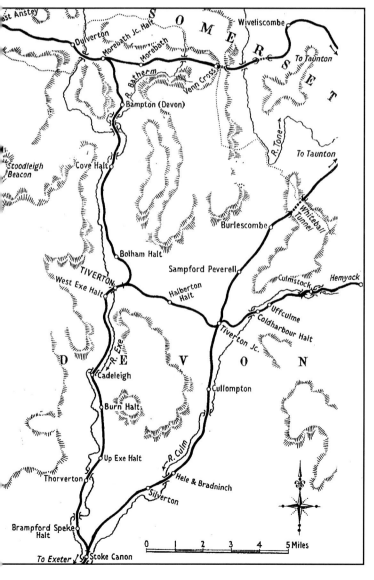

CONTENTS

Bampton	56
Bolham Halt	51
Brampford Speke Halt	14
Burn Halt	24
Cadeleigh	25
Coldharbour Halt	86
Cove Halt	52
Cowley Bridge Junction	7
Culmstock	94
Dulverton	65
Exeter St. Davids	1
Halberton Halt	73
Hemyock	106
Morebath Junction Halt	64
Morebath Junction	62
Stoke Canon	9
Thorverton	16
Tiverton	34
Tiverton Junction	75
Uffculme	89
Up Exe Halt	21
West Exe Halt	31
Whitehall Halt	102

I. Map of the routes in 1955.
(Railway Magazine)

GEOGRAPHICAL SETTING

Trains running north from the City of Exeter followed the River Exe closely to Tiverton, which was built at the confluence of the Exe with the River Lowman. The Exe was followed to within one mile of Bampton. Here the line joined the valley of the River Batherm to reach that town, from where it climbed steeply to Morebath Junction and then descended back into the Exe Valley, to arrive at Dulverton station. Much of the route was on Red Sandstone, but the part in the steep sided and well wooded valley of great charm was incised into Culm Measures. The limestone was of economic importance in the vicinity of Bampton.

The Tiverton to Tiverton Junction line was close to the western end of the Grand Western Canal, which linked Tiverton with Taunton until 1865. The branch line to Hemyock was entirely within the Culm Valley and was thus so named by the GWR. The route was flanked by gentle slopes, largely pasture, and had the Black Down Hills to the north. The River Culm continues south to join the River Exe south of Stoke Canon and is accompanied by the Taunton to Exeter main line to this day.

The journey from Exeter to Dulverton was entirely in Devon, apart from the final half mile which was in Somerset. The train climbed from 40 to nearly 500ft above sea level in almost 25 miles.

The maps are to the scale of 25 ins to 1 mile, unless shown otherwise.

II. Gradient profiles with mileages.

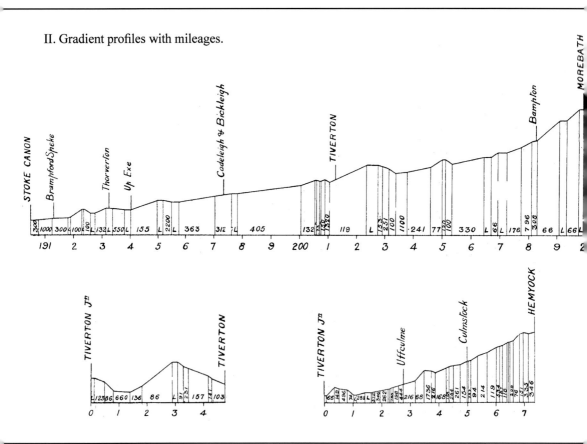

HISTORICAL BACKGROUND

The Bristol & Exeter Railway's main line between Taunton and Exeter was opened in stages and completed on 1st May 1844. The branch from Tiverton Junction to Tiverton came into use on 12th June 1848, the entire system being laid to the broad gauge of 7ft 0¼ ins. The BER also operated the Devon & Somerset Railway, which opened through Dulverton to reach Barnstaple on 1st November 1873. This line was converted to standard gauge in May 1881; the Tiverton branch followed on 29th June 1884.

The Exe Valley Railway Company obtained an Act on 30th June 1874 for the construction of a line from Stoke Canon to Tiverton. This company and the BER became part of the Great Western Railway in 1876.

The Tiverton & North Devon Railway began to build a line from Morebath Junction towards Tiverton in 1880 and this also came under the control of the GWR in due course. This route came into use on 1st August 1884 and the line south from Tiverton followed on 1st May 1885. Both were built to standard gauge.

The Culm Valley Light Railway was authorised under an Act of 15th May 1873 and the torturous line to Hemyock from Tiverton Junction was opened on 29th May 1876. It was built to standard gauge (the broad gauge main lines between Taunton and Exeter had received a third rail in March 1876). The branch was operated by the GWR, which purchased the undertaking in August 1880.

Nationalisation in 1948 resulted in the GWR becoming the Western Region of British Railways. Traffic continued to fall and passenger services were withdrawn thus: Tiverton Junction to Hemyock 9th September 1963, Exeter to Dulverton 7th October 1963 and Tiverton Junction to Tiverton 5th October 1964. The following sections were retained for some types of freight (detailed in the captions): Stoke Canon to Thorverton until 30th November 1966, Tiverton Junction to Tiverton until 5th June 1967 and Tiverton Junction to Hemyock until 1st November 1975.

PASSENGER SERVICES

Exe Valley

The initial service when the line opened between Tiverton and Dulverton comprised four trains, weekdays only. This was increased to six when services were extended to Exeter, a frequency that was maintained until 1915. The wartime reduction to four continued until 1923, when six were once again provided.

A major improvement took place in July 1928, when twelve trains were operated between Exeter and Tiverton, eight of which continued to Dulverton. Sunday trains were introduced in 1926, south of Tiverton only. The initial two soon increased to three and five were operated from 1937, although frequency was lower in the Winter in many years.

Little changed until closure, although stops at some halts were reduced after 1955. In some years there was an extra train on one or two days in the week and one terminated at Bampton in latter years. There were some reductions during World War II and after.

In the final years, the last evening train from Tiverton to Exeter ran via the main line, so that Valley signal boxes could close early.

Tiverton Branch

There were 9 or 10 trips on weekdays, with usually four on Sundays, during the broad gauge era. Subsequently, the weekday figure was usually 12, although reductions were made during both World Wars.

There was little in the way of through running, although there were some through coaches to Exeter in the early years. Later, there were some examples of circular operation from Exeter, using the Exe Valley and the main line.

Culm Valley

Four trips were operated throughout, weekdays only, during the life of the branch, although there was an extra one in the first two years or so and only three after September 1958, when the evening train was withdrawn. A late morning journey between Tiverton Junction and Uffculme was added in 1925, this continuing until closure. An occasional extra on Saturdays appeared in some timetables, but passenger carriage was not a strong point on this branch.

Some minor variations to the general outline of services on the routes given above can be seen in the timetable extracts that follow.

TAUNTON, EXETER, DULVERTON, BARNSTAPLE, and ILFRACOMBE.—Great Western.

(Down and Up timetables, October 1905)

October 1905

EXETER, TIVERTON, and DULVERTON (Motor Cars—One class only).—Great Western.

A St. David's.　**S** Saturdays only.　**T** Tuesdays only, not calling at the Halt.
¶ "Halt" at Cove, between Tiverton and Bampton (Devon).

September 1925

TIVERTON JUNCTION and HEMYOCK—Great Western.

September 1925

EXETER, TIVERTON, and DULVERTON (Motor Cars—One class only).

D St. David's.

August 1928

TIVERTON JUNCTION and HEMYOCK
(Third class only)

Miles	Week Days only								Miles		Week Days only						
		am	am E	am	am	pm	pm	pm				am	am E	pm	pm	pm	pm
—	Tiverton Junction.. dep	8 45	1135	1135	404	305	0 7	5		—	Hemyock .. — dep	7 20	1030	..	3 0	5 55	7 55
2¼	Coldharbour Halt ..	8 54	1144	1144	413	314	0 16	7 14		1	Whitehall Halt ..	7 24	1034	..	3 5	6 0	8 0
2¾	Uffculme	8 57	1147	1147	416	317	0 19	7 17		2¼	Culmstock	7 31	1043	..	3 13	6 8	8 7
5	Culmstock	9 21	..	12 52	44	325	227	27		4¼	Uffculme	7 40	1053	1210	3 19	2 56	18 8 17
6¼	Whitehall Halt ..	9 30	..	2 13	55	0 5	357	35		5	Coldharbour Halt ..	7 43	1057	1213	153 3	3 06	22 8 20
7¼	Hemyock .. .. arr	9 42	..	2 20	55	357	40			7¼	Tiverton Junction.. arr	7 52	11 7	1228	1233 3	41 6	33 8 29

E Except Saturdays.　**S** Saturdays only.

June 1955

June 1955

TIVERTON JUNCTION and TIVERTON

(Third class only)

Miles		Week Days																				Suns.	
		am	am S	am E	am S	am E	am S	am E	am T	am	pm	pm	pm E	pm S	pm E	pm E	pm S	pm	pm	pm			
—	Tiverton Junction.. dep	7 25	8 10	8 15	8 50	9 2	9 30	9 40	1035	1125	1250	1 40	2 22	4 18	4 25	5 6	5 30	7 5	8 40	9 25	..	..	..
2¼	Halberton Halt..........	7 31	8 15	8 20	8 55	9 7	9 35	9 45	1040	1130	1255	1 45	2 27	4 23	4 30	5 11	5 35	7 10	8 45	9 30	....	....	....
4¾	Tiverton .. .. .. arr	7 38	8 22	8 27	9 2	9 14	9 42	9 52	1047	1137	1 2	1 52	2 34	4 30	4 37	5 18	5 42	7 17	8 52	9 37	..	..	..

Miles		Week Days																				Suns.	
		am	am	am S	am E	am S	am E	am E	am S	pm	pm	pm E	pm	pm S	pm E	pm	pm	pm	pm Z	pm Z	pm S	pm Z	
—	Tiverton .. .. .. dep	7 10	7 40	8 30	8 45	9 5	9 20	1055	11 5	1220	1 20	2 0	4 0	4 35	4 45	6 25	8 15	9 0	9E45	9S55	1020	8 50	..
2¼	Halberton Halt	7 17	7 47	8 36	8 51	9 11	9 26	11 1	11 11	1226	1 26	2 6	4 6	4 41	4 51	6 31	8 21	9 6	9E51	10S1	1026	8 56	....
4¾	Tiverton Junction.. arr	7 23	7 53	8 42	8 57	9 17	9 32	11 7	1117	1232	1 32	2 12	4 12	4 47	4 57	6 37	8 27	9 12	9E57	10S7	1032	9 2	..

June 1955

EXETER, TIVERTON and DULVERTON

(Third class only)

Miles		Week Days																	Sundays				
		am	am	am S	am E	am	pm S	am E	pm E	pm S	pm E	pm S	pm E	pm	pm U	pm	pm E	pm S	am	am	pm	pm	pm
—	Exeter (St. David's).. dep	6 10	6 30	7 50	755	9 45	..	1130	1 10	1 43	2 5	3 43	4 0	5 55	6 53	7 40	9 10	9 37	8 40	1015	4 2	6 15	7 54
3½	Stoke Canon	....	....	7 58	8 1	9 54	....	1140	1 16	1 50	....	....	....	6 1	6 58	....	....	....	....	....	....	....	....
4¾	Brampford Speke Halt ..	..	6 39	8 3	8 5	9 58	..	1145	1 21	1 53	2 18	3 55	4 8	6 4	7 3	7 49	9 21	9 49	8 50	1025	4 12	6 25	8 5
6¼	Thorverton	6 23	6 45	8 14	815	10 5	....	1155	1 27	1 59	2 24	4 1	4 14	6 10	7 9	7 57	9 26	9 54	8 55	1030	4 18	6 30	8 10
7	Up Exe Halt	..	6 47	8 18	818	..	..	..	1 30	2 2	..	4 4	4 16	6 12	7 12	..	..	..	8 58	1033	4 22	6 34	8 15
9	Burn (for Butterleigh) Halt	....	6 51	8 22	822	....	....	....	1 34	2 6	....	4 8	4 20	....	....	....	....	....	9 2	1037	4 25	6 38	8 19
10½	Cadeleigh	6 32	6 54	8 27	827	1014	..	12 4	1 40	2 9	2 33	4 11	4 24	6 19	7 19	8 6	9 35	10 3	9 6	1040	4 30	6 42	8 23
13½	West Exe Halt	....	7 2	8 34	834	1022	1210	1212	1 50	2 17	2 41	4 19	4 31	6 26	7 26	8 14	9 43	1011	9 14	1048	4 38	6 50	8 31
14¼	**Tiverton** ... ... arr	**6 41**	**7 5**	**8 37**	**837**	**1025**	**1212**	**1215**	**1 53**	**2 20**	**2 45**	**4 22**	**4 34**	**6 29**	**7 30**	**8 17**	**9 46**	**1013**	**9 18**	**1051**	**4 41**	**6 53**	**8 35**
	dep	**6 43**	**7 10**	**8 40**	**840**	**1027**	**1213**	**1224**	**1 55**	**2 22**	**2 50**	**4 24**	**4 36**	**6 32**	**7 38**	**8 19**	**9T47**	**1015**	....	....	....	....	....
16	Bolham Halt	6 48	7 14	8 45	844	1032	1217	1229	2 0	2 27	2 54	4 29	4 41	6 36	7 43	8 24	9T52	1020	..	..	..	..	..
19½	Cove Halt	6 55	7 21	8 51	851	1039	1224	1236	2 7	2 34	3 1	4 36	4 48	6 43	7 50	8 31	9T59	1027	....	....	....	....	....
21¼	Bampton (Devon)	6 59	7 30	8 56	856	1043	1228	1240	2 12	2 38	3 5	4 40	4 52	6 47	7 54	8 36	10T 3	1031	..	..	..	..	..
23	Morebath Junction Halt ..	....	7 37	9 1	9 1	1049	1234	1246	....	2 44	3 11	4 46	4 58	6 53	8 0	8 42	10T 8	1037	....	....	....	....	....
24¾	**Dulverton**.. .. .. arr	**7 8**	**7 41**	**9 5**	**9 5**	**1053**	**1238**	**1250**	..	**2 48**	**3 15**	**4 50**	**5 2**	**6 57**	**8 4**	**8 47**	**10T13**	**1041**	..	..	..	..	..

Miles		Week Days																	Sundays				
		am	am	am	am E	am S	pm S	pm E	pm E	pm S	pm E	pm	pm	pm U	pm E	pm E	pm S	pm S	am	am	pm	pm	pm
—	**Dulverton**.. .. .. dep	**7 15**	**8 10**	**9 35**	**1110**	**1130**	**1250**	**1 5**	..	**3 25**	**3 45**	**5 25**	**7 10**	**8 25**	**9 15**	..	**9 25**	..	..	..	..	..	..
1¾	Morebath Junction Halt ..	7 19	8 14	9 39	....	1134	1256	1 9	....	3 29	3 49	5 29	7 14	8 29	9 19	....	9 29	....	....	....	....	....	....
3½	Bampton (Devon)	7 29	8 19	9 44	1118	1139	1 0	1 13	2 30	3 33	3 54	5 33	7 18	8 37	9 23	..	9 33	..	..	..	..	..	..
5¼	Cove Halt	7 34	8 24	9 49	1122	1144	1 5	1 18	2 34	3 38	3 59	5 38	7 23	8 42	9 27	....	9 37	....	....	....	....	....	....
8¾	Bolham Halt	7 41	8 31	9 56	1129	1151	1 12	1 26	2 41	3 45	4 5	5 45	7 30	8 49	9 34	..	9 44	..	..	..	..	..	..
10½	**Tiverton** .... arr	**7 46**	**8 36**	**10 1**	**1135**	**1156**	**1 17**	**1 31**	**2 46**	**3 50**	**4 11**	**5 50**	**7 35**	**8 54**	**9 40**	....	**9 50**	....	....	....	....	....	....
	dep	**7 50**	**8 40**	**10 4**	**1136**	**1159**	**1 19**	**1 32**	**2 50**	**4 0**	**4 13**	**5 52**	**7 37**	**8 55**	..	**9 45**	..	**9 55**	**9 30**	**11 5**	**4 55**	**7 0**	**8 50**
11¼	West Exe Halt	7 56	8 42	10 5	1138	12 0	1 20	1 34	2 51	4 2	4 14	5 53	7 39	8 56	....	Via Tiverton Junction	....	Via Tiverton Junction	9 32	11 7	4 57	7 2	Via Tiverton Junction
14¼	Cadeleigh	8 4	8 50	1014	1145	..	1 28	1 42	2 59	4 10	4 23	6 0	7 46	9 3	..		..		9 40	1115	5 5	7 10	
15¾	Burn (for Butterleigh) Halt	8 7	....	....	....	....	1 31	1 45	....	4 15	4 27	....	....	....	....		....		9 44	1119	5 8	7 14	
17¾	Up Exe Halt	8 11	..	..	..	..	1 35	1 49	..	4 20	4 32	..	7 53	..	..		..		9 48	1123	5 13	7 19	
18½	Thorverton	8 16	8 59	1024	1154	....	1 38	1 53	3 8	4 22	4 34	6 11	7 56	9 8	....		....		9 51	1126	5 15	7 22	
20¼	Brampford Speke Halt ..	8 21	9 3	1029	1158	..	1 43	1 58	3 14	4 27	4 39	6 16	8 1	9 12	..		..		9 55	1130	5 20	7 27	
21¼	Stoke Canon	8 26	....	1032	....	....	1 46	2 3	3 17	4 31	4 42	6 19	8 4	....	....		....		....	....	....	....	
24¾	**Exeter** (St. David's).. arr	**8 35**	**9 13**	**1040**	**12 8**	..	**1 58**	**2 11**	**3 25**	**4 42**	**4 50**	**6 26**	**8 13**	**9 22**	..	**1025**	..	**1035**	**10 5**	**1140**	**5 30**	**7 35**	**9 40**

To add to the rural ambience of the Exe Valley, the line had two named autocoaches. Usually only Pullman Car passengers had such consideration. Hopefully, few considered this one to refer to a medical condition. The second was *Wren*, but the others in a batch of 15 in 1951 remained nameless. (A.E.Bennett)

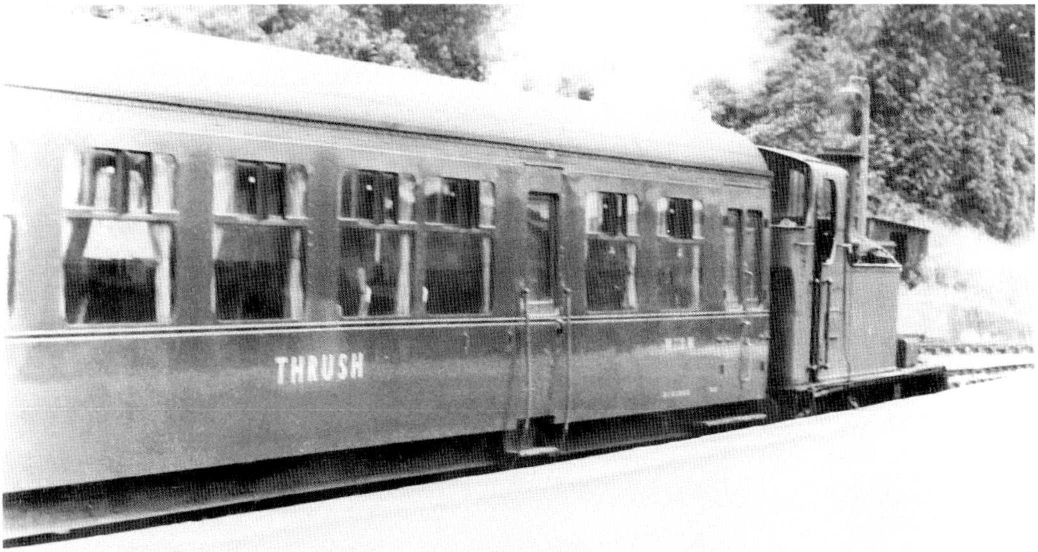

1.
Exeter to
Dulverton

EXETER
ST. DAVIDS

III. The 1932 survey shows the arrangement of through passenger lines since the rebuilding of 1911-14. Through goods lines were provided between the goods shed and the engine shed. The first station had only one long platform, up and down trains being accommodated at opposite ends of it.

1. The second station of 1860 is seen from the east after 1905 (as a tramcar is visible) but before 1911 (as the main roof is complete). Trams ceased to run in 1931 and the cab road canopy (left) was removed in 1939. (Lens of Sutton)

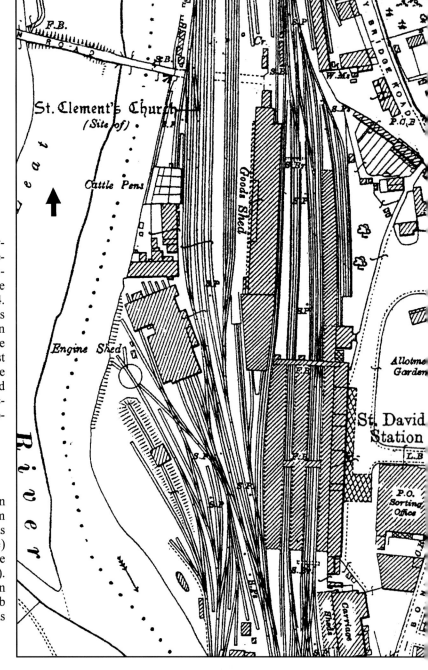

2. The overall roof was dismantled in favour of individual platform canopies and luggage lifts were provided in the stone towers. This 1921 panorama includes the goods shed (right) and the bay platform (centre). The dock on the left was not for passenger use. (LGRP/NRM)

3. An unusual locomotive photographed at Exeter on 25th May 1929 was no. 1308 *Lady Margaret*. It appears in our *Branch Line to Looe* as it was built for the Liskeard & Looe Railway. This became part of the GWR and the locomotive was transferred to work the branch to Hemyock in 1929, albeit briefly. It had been built by Andrew Barclay in 1902 and lasted until 1948. (H.C.Casserley)

4. The 4500 class small Prairie 2-6-2Ts made fewer appearances on Exe Valley trains than the 0-4-2Ts. No. 4589 was recorded in March 1959, bound for Dulverton. About 15 members of this class were fitted for push-pull working in 1953. The station lighting is in transition from gas to electric. (H.Cowan)

5. Displaying its Exeter shed code (83C), 0-6-0PT no. 3794 stands in the bay platform (no. 2) on 19th September 1960. Dulverton trains normally used this platform; 40 years later it was still in use, but only occasionally and then by the Barnstaple service. (N.L.Browne)

Transport in Exeter is illustrated further in these companion
Middleton Press albums:
*Branch Lines to Exmouth, Branch Line to Moretonhampstead,
Exeter to Barnstaple, Exeter to Newton Abbot,
Exeter to Tavistock, Exeter and Taunton Tramways,
Taunton to Exeter* **and** *Yeovil to Exeter.*

6. No. 1451 is waiting to leave from no. 2 for Tiverton at 12.45pm on 15th June 1963. Also featured is Middle Box, which was in use from 4th July 1914 until 1st April 1985. Further north was East Box and Riverside Box, which were opened in 1942 and 1943, respectively, in connection with a new marshalling yard for wartime traffic. The locomotive partially obscuring the goods transfer shed is a class W 2-6-4T; it is waiting in a short siding to assist the next train to Exeter Central requiring a banker. (E.Wilmshurst)

7. Having passed Riverside Yard, no. 7761 approaches the junction with the 5.48pm to Dulverton on 9th June 1960. The yard's initial seven sidings were increased to 13 in 1966, these being in addition to the two goods running lines seen on the right. (S.C.Nash)

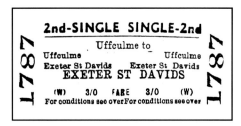

8. A northward view of the junction on 27th October 1960 has the Barnstaple line beyond the signal box and the main line under water. The track normally passed *over* the River Exe twice in the two miles to Stoke Canon. The box was very busy in the Summer of 1962, with over 200 trains on each weekday. Similar flooding occurred exactly 40 years after the photograph was taken. The box closed on 1st April 1985. (D.Edmund/S.P.Derek)

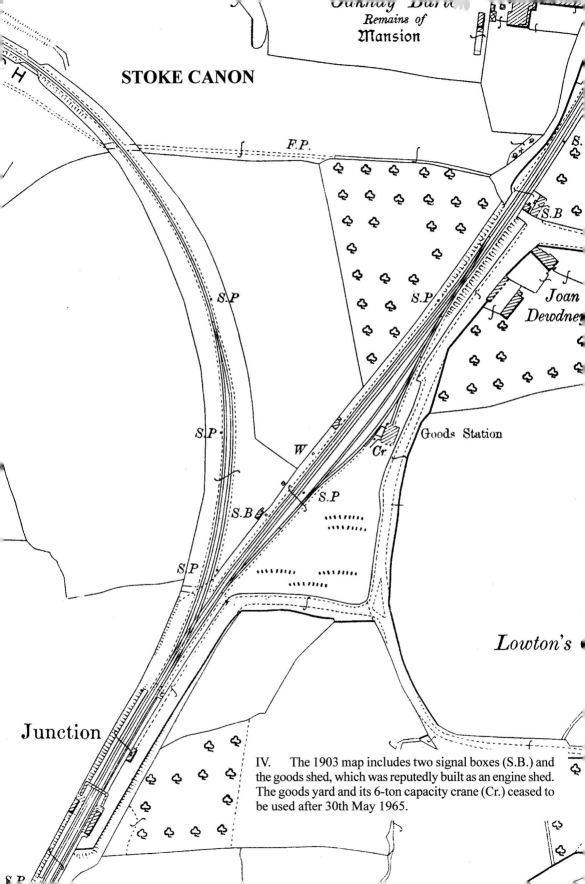

STOKE CANON

Remains of
Mansion

H

F.P.

S.

S.B

S.P.

S.P.

*Joan
Dewdney*

S.P.

S.P

W.

Goods Station

Cr.

S.P

S.B

S.P

Lowton's

Junction

IV.   The 1903 map includes two signal boxes (S.B.) and
the goods shed, which was reputedly built as an engine shed.
The goods yard and its 6-ton capacity crane (Cr.) ceased to
be used after 30th May 1965.

S P

9. An autotrain is being propelled onto the down main line in October 1924; the junction box is visible behind the coaches. Prior to 1894, the platforms were on opposite sides of the level crossing, the signal box for which is in the background, beyond the goods yard. (Lens of Sutton)

10.   Another northward view also includes the junction box, which closed on 19th July 1931. The platforms and buildings were cleared away soon after to allow the construction of a new station with two through lines and three platform lines. (Mowat coll.)

11.   The new station came into use in March 1932 and is seen from the north soon after. Note that the branch platform on the right is half the length of the other two. The building was in commercial use in 2000. (British Railways)

12.   No. 5546 waits with a train for Dulverton in May 1959. The footbridge spans four tracks without any stanchions. The train is standing at the island platform; this loop line was signalled for reversible running. The station closed on 13th June 1960, in advance of the branch, but the signal box (right) was in use until 3rd May 1964. It was commissioned in July 1931. (H.Cowan)

13.   The branch remained in use as far as Thorverton for grain traffic until 30th November 1966. Empties are arriving behind no. 4655 on 1st May 1965. The train will stop at the site of the station, reverse up the remaining part of the up loop (third track from the camera) to Stoke Canon Crossing Signal Box and then use the crossover to the down main line. (R.A.Lumber)

V.   The 1946 revision at 1 ins to 1 mile includes the location of the junction and also the two halts north thereof.

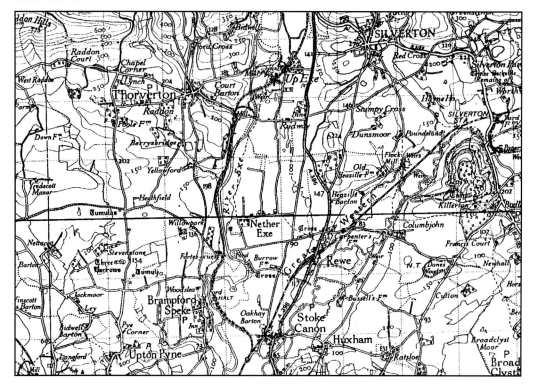

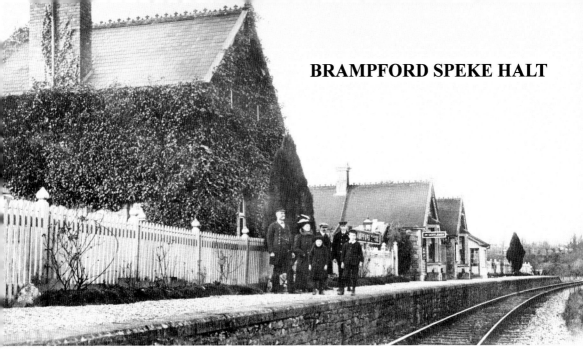

BRAMPFORD SPEKE HALT

14.　This postcard view dates from about 1910, the ivy having had around 25 years to mature on the station house. As a wartime economy measure, the station was closed in 1915-17. A staff of two was recorded in 1913 and 1923. Beyond the main building is the signal box, which had contained a seven-lever frame until closure in 1907. There had been a two-armed post at the far end of the platform. (Lens of Sutton)

15.　The house had been cleaned by the time that 2-6-2T no. 4548 was recorded bound for Exeter in May 1958. The station had been downgraded to a halt in 1923, in which year receipts were £246, which included sale of 12 season tickets. On Summer Sundays, a 4500 class 2-6-2T and up to five coaches (including first class) were provided for the 9.20am from Tiverton as it ran through to Newton Abbot with day-trippers to the coast. There had also been a signal box at Fortesque Crossing, half a mile to the north until 1907, when it was reduced to a ground frame with fixed distant signals. (H.Cowan)

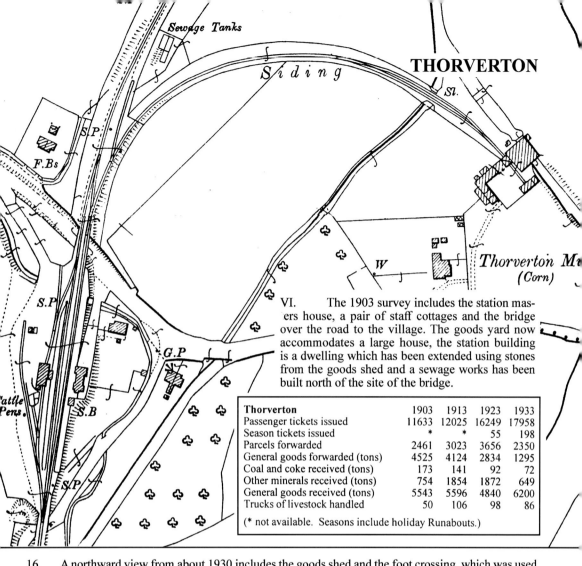

THORVERTON

Sewage Tanks

Siding

St.

S.P

F.Bs

S.P

W

Thorverton Mi
(Corn)

G.P

Cattle Pens.

S.B

S.P

VI.   The 1903 survey includes the station mas-
ers house, a pair of staff cottages and the bridge
over the road to the village. The goods yard now
accommodates a large house, the station building
is a dwelling which has been extended using stones
from the goods shed and a sewage works has been
built north of the site of the bridge.

Thorverton	1903	1913	1923	1933
Passenger tickets issued	11633	12025	16249	17958
Season tickets issued	*	*	55	198
Parcels forwarded	2461	3023	3656	2350
General goods forwarded (tons)	4525	4124	2834	1295
Coal and coke received (tons)	173	141	92	72
Other minerals received (tons)	754	1854	1872	649
General goods received (tons)	5543	5596	4840	6200
Trucks of livestock handled	50	106	98	86
(* not available. Seasons include holiday Runabouts.)				

16.   A northward view from about 1930 includes the goods shed and the foot crossing, which was used
by passengers. Its danger was reduced in 1923 when autotrains were introduced and the drivers of down
trains had a better view ahead. (Mowat coll.)

17.   This southward panorama is also from the 1930s, during which decade there was a staff of six. Camping coaches were located in the goods yard here during the Summers of 1936-39. The box had 20 levers, two of which were spare. (Stations UK)

18.   The tracery of the loading gauge brackets can be admired as no. 1462 enters the loop on 30th July 1959 with corridor coaches forming the 5.30pm from Dulverton. There had been a short siding on the left in the early years; it is shown on the map. (R.A.Lumber)

19.　　Autocoaches nos. W244 and W250 formed the 1.5pm from Dulverton on 28th July 1962. Although passenger trains ceased in October 1963, the signal box was not closed until 6th April 1964. The station was busy to the end, as there was no bus route nearby. (S.P.Derek)

20.　　Owing to the curvature of the track, the up advance starter signal was sited well away from the track, near the left border of the picture, which is from 8th June 1963. The 5.48pm from Exeter St. Davids is departing, while the 5.15 from Dulverton stands at the down platform. In the goods yard is the 5-ton crane and some condemned wagons, while grain wagons stand beyond the gate on the 1898 private siding of E.J.Coombe Ltd. Their mill (right) was served until 30th November 1966, imported grain being brought in from Avonmouth for milling. (P.W.Gray)

UP EXE HALT

21.   As at Brampford Speke, there was a staff of two until the station was demoted to become a halt on 1st October 1923. This northward view shows it soon afterwards, when it had become a residence. The signal box had eight levers and had been designated a ground frame in 1907, as had Up Exe South Crossing. The white hut was provided in 1923 as a waiting shelter. (Stations UK)

22.   The 2.8pm from Exeter St. Davids departs north on 22nd September 1962. Several trains passed through non-stop after a timetable revision in 1954. The name was "Up Exe & Silverton" until 1st May 1905, although Silverton had its own station on the main line. (S.P.Derek)

23.   The stone built structure remained in use as a dwelling after closure and was photographed in 1965 from the site of North Crossing. This peaceful location is close to one of the many meanders of the River Exe. (Stations UK)

BURN HALT

24.   The halt opened on 26th January 1929, but was little used owing to the very small local population and the close proximity of the buses on the A396. This northward view is from 1960. Six years earlier, the service had been reduced to peak hours only. The suffix states "for Butterleigh". (Stations UK)

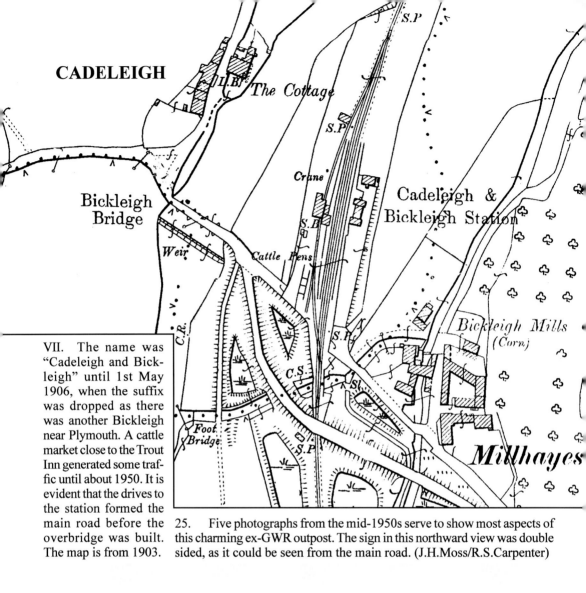

CADELEIGH

The Cottage

Bickleigh Bridge

Weir

Cattle Pens

Crane

Cadeleigh & Bickleigh Station

Bickleigh Mills (Corn)

Foot Bridge

Millhayes

VII. The name was "Cadeleigh and Bickleigh" until 1st May 1906, when the suffix was dropped as there was another Bickleigh near Plymouth. A cattle market close to the Trout Inn generated some traffic until about 1950. It is evident that the drives to the station formed the main road before the overbridge was built. The map is from 1903.

25. Five photographs from the mid-1950s serve to show most aspects of this charming ex-GWR outpost. The sign in this northward view was double sided, as it could be seen from the main road. (J.H.Moss/R.S.Carpenter)

26.   The goods office was at the north end of the shed and both were attractively finished with ornate ridge tiles to match the main building. The internal crane was supplemented by one of 6-ton capacity in the yard. After closure the site became a highways depot for Devon County Council and the buildings were used as stores. (J.H.Moss/R.S.Carpenter)

Cadeleigh	1903	1913	1923	1933
Passenger tickets issued	10084	8892	6560	6756
Season tickets issued	*	*	35	81
Parcels forwarded	2187	4996	3752	1486
General goods forwarded (tons)	895	1139	848	642
Coal and coke received (tons)	43	22	16	9
Other minerals received (tons)	935	2103	2243	1646
General goods received (tons)	2131	2390	2326	2146
Trucks of livestock handled	54	62	169	61

(* not available. Seasons include holiday Runabouts.)

27.   The ornamentation was extended to the barge boards and the chimney stacks. There was no entrance at the back of the building; all passengers passed through the gate on the right and the porch. Once therein they could turn right into the general waiting room, at the rear of which was the ladies room, or turn left into the ticket office. The lean-to housed the gents, the doorway being on the left. (J.H.Moss/R.S.Carpenter)

28.   The cattle pen can be seen above the lady's right shoulder. It originally had its own short siding from the goods loop. As at Thorverton, passengers used the foot crossing. Notable in the goods outward list was timber and sugar beet. (J.H.Moss/R.S.Carpenter)

29.   The approach road passed over a stream and ended at the south elevation. Beyond the station building is the two-storey house for the station master. There was a staff of three throughout the 1920s and 30s. (H.C.Casserley)

30.   The 10.25am from Exeter St. Davids drifts into the up platform on 11th May 1963 and the signalman waits to collect the electric token. This equipment had been in use since 1948; prior to that the key staff had provided single line safety. (S.P.Derek)

DEVON RAILWAY CENTRE

The site and buildings were purchased from the DCC in February 1997. The structures were renovated to the condition shown and two 1956 Mk I coaches were acquired to house model railway displays. An 0-4-0 standard gauge 1952 Baguley diesel locomotive named Boris operates occasionally. (DRC)

An extensive two-foot gauge system came into use in 1998. The steam outline of Ivor was created elsewhere on a Motor Rail diesel of 1944. There were eight other industrial locomotives present at the end of 2000, the goods shed in the background housing them, plus a wide range of historic stock. (DRC)

Steam returned to the Exe Valley in July 2000 when the 1922 Kerr Stuart Peter Pan visited the line, it normally residing on the Leighton Buzzard Railway. It worked for the DCC prior to preservation and arrived with one of that county's wagons. It is seen at the halt near the north end of the railway. (P.Nicholson)

Track diagram - not to scale. The overall length is about half a mile.

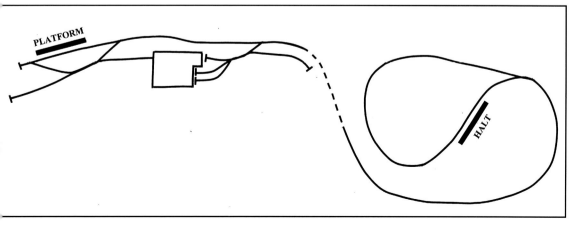

WEST EXE HALT

31.   The halt opened on 9th March 1928 and served the western residential area of Tiverton. An up train is approaching the original part of the platform in July 1958. Oil lamps were provided by the guard as necessary. There was a small ticket office, in use at busy times only.
(R.M.Casserley)

These tickets were issued from a hand-held rack.

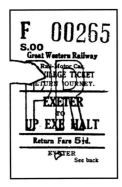

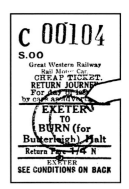

32.   The halt was often extremely busy, notably on Summer Sundays with day-trippers to the coast, thus the platform had to be doubled in length in 1937. In addition to all the Exeter trains, the 1928 timetable showed a train terminating here at 10.07am after a two minute journey from Tiverton, plus one starting at 7.5pm for a one minute trip to the town. They were discontinued in 1929! (R.M.Casserley)

WEST OF TIVERTON

33.   On leaving West Exe Halt, trains passd over the A396 and then over the River Exe on this fine four-arched stone structure. Class 5700 0-6-0PT no. 3659 is seen with the 12.48pm from Exeter St. Davids on 13th October 1962. On Saturdays in the 1950s, there was one train from Dulverton that terminated at West Exe Halt at 12.0 noon and returned at 12.10. (S.P.Derek)

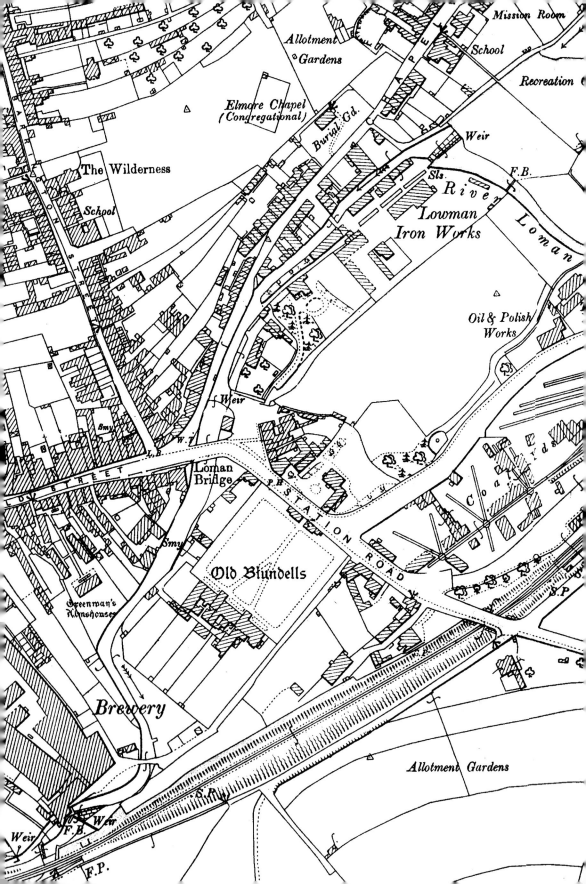

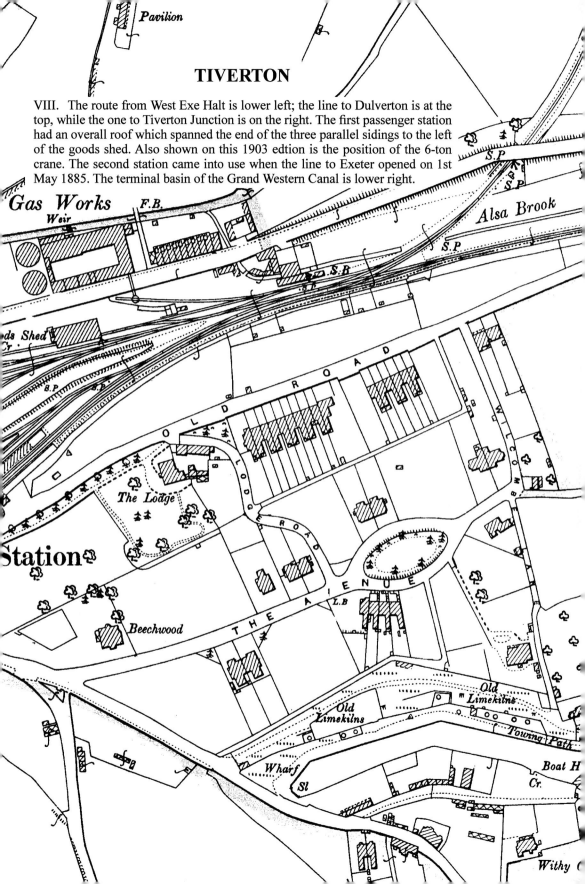

TIVERTON

VIII.   The route from West Exe Halt is lower left; the line to Dulverton is at the top, while the one to Tiverton Junction is on the right. The first passenger station had an overall roof which spanned the end of the three parallel sidings to the left of the goods shed. Also shown on this 1903 edtion is the position of the 6-ton crane. The second station came into use when the line to Exeter opened on 1st May 1885. The terminal basin of the Grand Western Canal is lower right.

Gas Works

Weir   F.B.

Alsa Brook

S.P.

S.P.

S.P.

S.B.

S.P.

ds Shed

Cr.

S.P.   S.P.

OLD   ROAD

LODGE   ROAD

WILLOW

The Lodge

Station

ROAD

THE   AVENUE

Beechwood

L.B.

Old
Limekilns

Old
Limekilns

Towing Path

Wharf

Sl

Boat H

Cr.

Withy C

34.   This northward view is from between 1923, when autotrains were introduced on the Exe Valley route, and May 1931, when the down bay came into use. It was created by removing the fence in the distance. There was an entrance near the far stanchion on the right. (LGRP/NRM)

Tiverton	1903	1913	1923	1933
Passenger tickets issued	76374	76366	70298	50471
Season tickets issued	*	*	150	738
Parcels forwarded	44341	51841	42669	53228
General goods forwarded (tons)	9283	11048	11347	8561
Coal and coke received (tons)	5686	5602	4945	10577
Other minerals received (tons)	7569	10536	6116	3790
General goods received (tons)	18333	20972	22500	27026
Trucks of livestock handled	986	1007	839	531

(* not available. Seasons include holiday Runabouts.)

35.   Standing in the new down bay is the branch train for Tiverton Junction, which was known as the "Tivvy Bumper". Note that the platforms had been lengthened, although the trains were not. (Stations UK)

36.   Another photograph from the 1930s emphasises the importance of the station which was provided for what was once Devon's third largest town. However, it did not expand to the extent of Exeter and Plymouth. (Stations UK)

37.   The generous width of the stairs and the elegant main entrance arch are evident in this 1935 record of a train arriving from Exeter. The seven-lever South Box had been situated near the signal until 1912. The arm carrying an "S" was for shunting movements. (Stations UK)

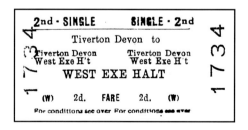

38.   The splendid array of signals can be studied as no. 1440 propels an autocoach from Tiverton Junction into the down bay on 30th May 1959. North Box had stood near the hut in the distance until 1912. It had 25 levers. (S.C.Nash)

39.   No. 4589 was captured shunting stock for the 5.22pm to Exeter on the same day. This "Prairie Tank" was fitted to work with autocoaches. The bus garage is that of Devon General. (S.C.Nash)

40. The shadows lengthen on the same day as no. 1471 glides in with the 5.30pm from Dulverton. It was uncommon to see a locomotive at this end of a down train. No. 1440 is in the bay with the "Tivvy Bumper". (S.C.Nash)

41. The signal box came into use on 6th May 1912 and was fitted with a 40-lever frame. Also included is the short white post of the tablet carrier, the tall black shed of the permanent way gang and the tapered post carrying the down bay starting signal. The up bay did not have one, only a ground signal, and was seldom in use for passenger trains. (I.D.Beale)

42.   The station building and approach road are included in this 1960 panorama. The through platform lines were retained after passenger closure to enable locomotives to run round goods trains. (I.D.Beale)

Other views of Tiverton can be found in *Taunton to Exeter*.

43.   A closer look at the prospective passenger's perspective reveals some excellent architectural detailing, such as the chimney pots and the finials. The Ford Popular represents a nail in the railway coffin under preparation. (I.D.Beale)

44.   Five more photographs from 1960 help to create the ambience of this often busy junction, which had a staff of 30 in 1930 increasing to 38 in 1958. The gas lights and Scammell mechanical horse add to the period flavour. (I.D.Beale)

45.   A few minutes later and no. 1450 passes the signalman who offers the token for the next stage of its journey to Dulverton. Electric tokens were introduced to Tiverton Junction in 1932, but not until 1948 on the route northwards. (I.D.Beale)

46.   The driver's view from the down bay includes the Dulverton line curving left round the wagon, the 10mph speed restriction sign and the single line to Tiverton Junction on the right. (I.D.Beale)

47.   No. 1471 waits in the up bay with freight, while no. 1440 shows evidence of maximum boiler pressure prior to departure for Dulverton. The goods yard remained open until 5th June 1967. (R.S.Carpenter)

48.   Water supply features can be studied in this view, which includes the tank, one of the three columns and fire devil to prevent it freezing. The grill on the platform ramp collected surplus water after filling was finished. (C.L.Caddy/J.W.House)

49.   Autocoaches were introduced on the "Tivvy Bumper" in 1932, following completion of this bay. No longer was it necessary to run round after each trip and the track revision at that time meant that trains could arrive from the north and east simultaneously. (L.W.Rowe)

50.   No. 1442 was purchased by Lord Amory who presented it to Tiverton Museum in 1965. It stood on a plinth in Blundells Road, where it was photographed with a new Bristol RE bus (Devon General no. 228) in 1973. It was moved inside the museum in 1978. (C.L.Caddy)

BOLHAM HALT

51.   Opened on 23rd April 1928, the halt was photographed a few weeks before closure. The shelter faced west and so was of limited value in the prevailing winds. Although the community was small, the halt was quite well used. (E.Wilmshurst)

COVE HALT

52.   The five-wagon public siding in the background was provided when the line opened, but the halt did not open until 9th June 1924. The adjacent quarry, seen in this 1956 northward view, did not use the railway. The siding had a southward spur for two wagons until 1923. (H.C.Casserley)

53.   No. 5555 draws into the platform with the 3.20pm from Bampton to collect one lady and her pram on 20th October 1962. The 13-lever signal box became a ground frame in 1923 and survived, along with the adjacent crossing keepers house, in private ownership after the line closed. (S.P.Derek)

54.　　Initially the platform was at ballast level and the folding steps on the autocoaches were swung out. When the level was raised, a classic GWR Pagoda shelter appeared, the only one on the route. No. 1450 is departing southwards at the rear of its train on 15th June 1963. (E.Wilmshurst)

SOUTH OF BAMPTON

55.　　The scenic pleasures were particularly delightful in this narrow valley, the line crossing the Exe near its confluence with the River Batherm. No. 1471 propels the 3.35 Dulverton to Exeter St. Davids over the lattice girders on 30th July 1963. (S.P.Derek)

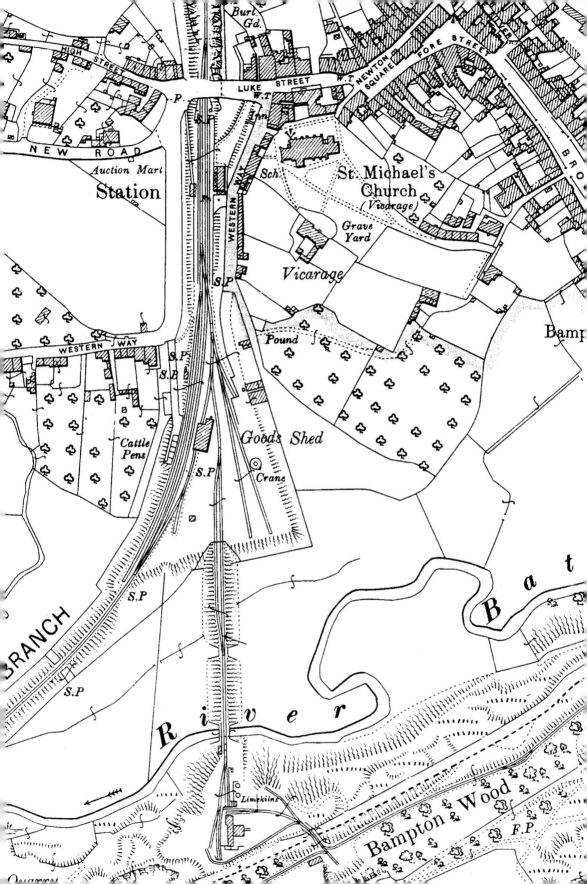

BAMPTON

Mill Leat Lane

Allotment
Gardens

Town Mill
(Corn)

F.B.
Millhead

Old Limekiln

W.T

BRITON STREET

Tiverton Hotel

Police
Station

W.T
L.B

IX.   The 1903 survey in-
dicates that the line to the
quarry passes over the river
and has a loop across which
there are gates.

Kersdown Quarry
(Disused)

1401

Old Limekiln

Old Limekil

dge

Stony

56.   The goods yard had a 5-ton crane and a connection to the quarry seen in the background of this 1948 photograph. It was from the siding to the left of the goods shed and was in use from 1898 to about 1950. The last producer of lime and limestone was J.W.Scott & Sons. (D.Clayton)

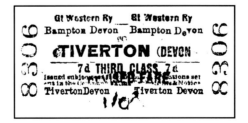

57.   No. 1451 was photographed in fine condition, unlike the station which had defective ridge tiles. These 41 ton locomotives were designed in 1932 and were quite sprightly, although limited to 35mph in the Exe Valley. Crowds were not a feature of this station, as the local population was only about 1500. (M.Dart coll.)

58.   No. 1471 has a van attached to its two coaches for its journey to Dulverton. The signal box is out of view, almost opposite the goods shed. All freight from here had been routed via Dulverton since September 1954. (R.C.Riley)

59.   Featured here are the tall posts on which pressurised oil lamps were hung at night. Also evident is the up platform shelter. After closure, all was demolished and the cutting was largely infilled. In the final years, the 4.25pm from Exeter St. Davids terminated here at 5.23, Mondays to Fridays. It returned at 6.10, missing four of the five halts. (N.L.Browne)

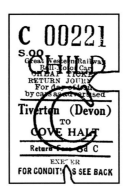

C 00221

S.00

Great Western Railway
Rail Road Car
CHEAP TICKET
RETURN JOURNEY
For day of issue
by car as advertised

Tiverton (Devon)
TO
COVE HALT

Return Fare 5d C

EXETER
FOR CONDITIONS SEE BACK

60.   No. 1462 departs with the unusually long 9.45am from Dulverton on Saturday 4th August 1962. It was Bank Holiday weekend. The spacious signal box had 22 levers, seven of which were spare. Industrial premises now cover this area. (S.P.Derek)

61.   This panorama completes our study of the facilities as it includes the loading dock and the crane. Only the cattle pen has not been seen; it was close to the signal box. The autumn Pony Fair produced some extra traffic here. (S.J.Dickson)

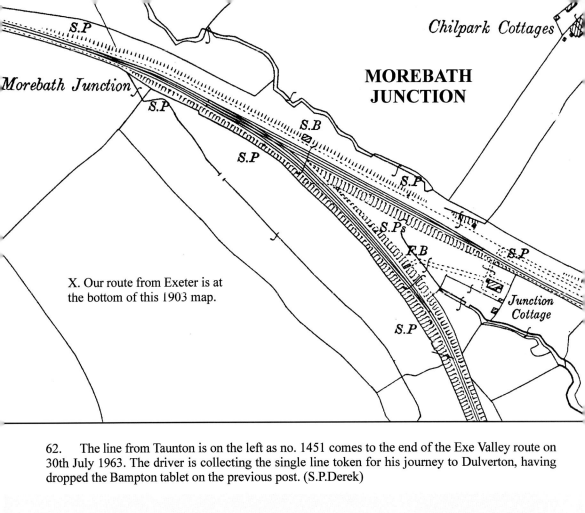

Morebath Junction

Chilpark Cottages

MOREBATH JUNCTION

S.P

S.P

S.B

S.P

S.P

S.P.s

F.B

S.P

S.P

Junction Cottage

X. Our route from Exeter is at the bottom of this 1903 map.

62.   The line from Taunton is on the left as no. 1451 comes to the end of the Exe Valley route on 30th July 1963. The driver is collecting the single line token for his journey to Dulverton, having dropped the Bampton tablet on the previous post. (S.P.Derek)

63.   No. 1450 is propelling the 1.5pm Saturdays-only Dulverton to Exeter St. Davids over the junction on 7th September 1963, one month before the route closed. The signal box and loop remained in use until 29th April 1964. Morebath station was over one mile east of the junction. (R.A.Lumber)

MOREBATH JUNCTION HALT

64.   The halt opened on 1st December 1928 and was in use until 3rd October 1966. It was close to the junction (the box is in the distance), but a half-mile walk to the village centre. The can is for the signalman's drinking water; another is visible in picture 57. (Stations UK)

DULVERTON

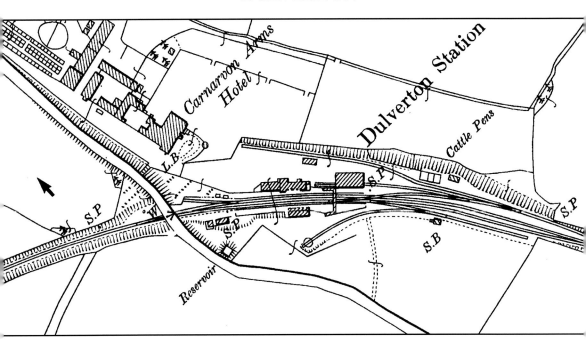

XI.   The 1903 survey shows the first position of the signal box and the original approach to the turntable. Brushford catttle market is top left; Dulverton was more than two miles distant and served by a bus connection.

65.   When the line opened in 1873, sidings were provided only on the left. One on the south side followed soon after the 1881 gauge conversion. The others, together with the loop line and third platform face, came into use on 6th January 1910. (Mowat coll.)

66.   The panorama towards Taunton includes part of the Exe Valley. The line dropped at 1 in 88 into it and then climbed out of it at 1 in 60 and 1 in 58. The building on the right contained toilets and a waiting room. (J.H.Moss/R.S.Carpenter)

67.   Looking towards Barnstaple, we glimpse the short dock siding, which could accommodate two wagons, usually horseboxes. The table of a weighing machine is set into the platform, lower right. (J.H.Moss/R.S.Carpenter)

68.   No. 1451 has reached the end of its journey on 22nd August 1958 and the guard checks for lost property. The station received electric lighting in 1950 and a 6-ton crane (right) in 1937. Its predecessor had been of 5-ton capacity. (A.E.Bennett)

**Other views of this station and of
Morebath Junction can be seen in**
Taunton to Barnstaple.
(Middleton Press)

69.   No. 1420 enters the "Back Road" in August 1959 and approaches the token catcher. The route had electric train staffs until 1937. The signal arm is endorsed BAY. (R.S.Carpenter coll.)

70.   The 2.24pm Barnstaple to Taunton was hauled by 4300 class 2-6-0 no. 7326 on 16th August 1962 and no. 1450 was on the 2.8pm from Exeter. The 53-lever signal box came into use on 6th January 1910. The goods yard closed on 6th July 1964. (L.W.Rowe)

71.   Seen almost 12 months later, the same locomotive is about to have its tanks replenished. The turntable (right) dates from 1881, but the direction of access to it was reversed in 1910. It was little used after the introduction of autotrains in 1923. There was a staff of 10 at that time here. (A.E.Bennett)

72.   The 12.30pm to Exeter St. Davids departed from the up platform, unusually, on 30th July 1963. The signal on the left explains why the trains in pictures 68 and 70 have stopped near the east end of the platform. That one was taken out of use in Aril 1964 and the down platform followed on 31st July 1966, when the signal box also closed. The entire route succumbed on 3rd October of that year. (S.P.Derek)

2. Tiverton to Tiverton Junction
HALBERTON HALT

73.   The halt was situated about half way along the branch, but it did not come into use until 5th December 1927. Running towards Tiverton Junction in 1960, we can observe that provision was made for double track. An entrepreneur leased the unused land and laid out two one-mile long rows of apple trees. (I.D.Beale)

74.   The halt was well patronised and almost all trains stopped, as it was close to the village. A little to the west was a two-arch aqueduct carrying the Grand Western Canal over the line. This section still contains water. (C.L.Caddy)

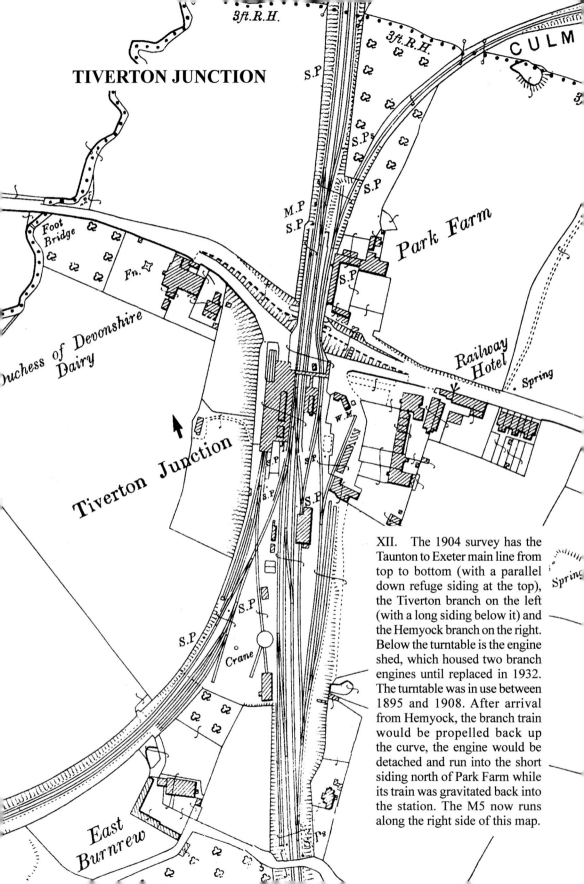

TIVERTON JUNCTION

3ft.R.H.

3ft.R.H.

CULM

S.P

S.P

S.Ps

S.P

Park Farm

M.P
S.P

S.P

Foot
Bridge

Fn.

Railway
Hotel

Spring

Duchess of Devonshire
Dairy

W.M

S.P

S.P

Tiverton Junction

S.P

S.P

S.P

S.P

S.P

Spring

S.P

Crane

East
Burnrew

XII. The 1904 survey has the Taunton to Exeter main line from top to bottom (with a parallel down refuge siding at the top), the Tiverton branch on the left (with a long siding below it) and the Hemyock branch on the right. Below the turntable is the engine shed, which housed two branch engines until replaced in 1932. The turntable was in use between 1895 and 1908. After arrival from Hemyock, the branch train would be propelled back up the curve, the engine would be detached and run into the short siding north of Park Farm while its train was gravitated back into the station. The M5 now runs along the right side of this map.

75.　A northward panorama includes the Tiverton branch platform on the left. Everything was swept away during a major reconstruction in 1932, when two fast lines were provided between the platform lines. The van on the left was detached from a morning up train and attached to a later train, the branch engine undertaking the task. There was a staff of 27 in the early 1930s. (British Railways)

76.　The branch train smoke lingers in the roof, as the autotrain disappears round the curve. Before the introduction of this type of train here in 1932, the coaches used to be propelled up the steeply inclined siding on the right. After the engine had run out of the train shed, the coaches would be rolled back into the platform under gravity. (G.N.Southenden)

77.   The new station is seen from the north after the footbridge had received a roof in about 1946. The Hemyock branch is on the left, together with its home signals. The A373 passes under all seven tracks. The first station was known as "Tiverton Road" until the Tiverton branch opened on 12th June 1848. (H.C.Casserley)

78.　　Looking from the south in 1959, we have the line from Tiverton on the far left and a complete panorama of all the 1932 structures. The signal box had 120 levers; the number in use was steadily reduced during the 1960s until the box became a simple block post controlling two goods loops. It lasted until 1st March 1986. (Stations UK)

79.　　No. 1449 has just arrived from Hemyock and is taking water on 23rd July 1958. The tank on the right fed three columns. It had been supplied by steam power until 1928, an oil engine until 1945 and electrically thereafter. The line on the right served the goods shed, to the east of which there were eight sidings. (R.C.Riley)

80.   The 8.15am to Tiverton departs on 22nd August 1958, propelled by no. 1469. The sidings on the left were used for the reception and despatch of branch goods trains. (A.E.Bennett)

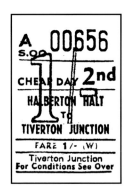

81.   In the left background in this northward view from the footbridge are petrol storage tanks. The "Park" sidings had been provided for the Air Ministry in November 1943 and were used by Esso latterly, closing in April 1983. The locomotives are (from left to right) nos. 1451, 4955, 6815 and 5924 and are seen on 1st July 1960. (R.S.Carpenter)

82.   Looking back from the platform ramp featured in the previous view, we have no. 1450 in view. Forty years later, this engine was working on the Gloucestershire Warwickshire Railway. On the right is the "Butter Platform", constructed specially for this traffic in 1932. Speed of despatch was important in pre-refrigeration days. (I.D.Beale)

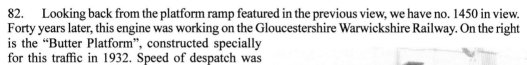

83.　The signals are to the right of the single line to Tiverton in this 1961 view of the layout behind the signal box. The line on the left connects with the up platform road and diverging from it is the siding to the pig pens. In the centre is the engine shed, which was in use from 1932 to October 1964. (R.S.Carpenter)

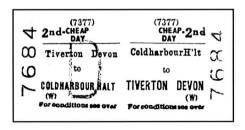

84.   No. 1451 departs for Hemyock on 15th June 1962, while a connecting train stands at the down platform. By that time, this track had flat-bottom rail, while the others still had bull-head. The connection on the left was removed in 1964. (R.C.Riley)

85.   Diesels were not used on the passenger services featured in this album, except during the final week in the Exe Valley. No. D6337 is seen leaving the goods shed road, at 15.50 on 30th April 1969, to collect milk tankers from Hemyock. The goods yard closed on 8th May 1967 and passenger services ceased on 12th May 1986, when Tiverton Parkway opened, more than a mile to the north. The site was cleared, but the two loops and two down sidings were retained. (R.A.Lumber)

3. Tiverton Junction to Hemyock
COLDHARBOUR HALT

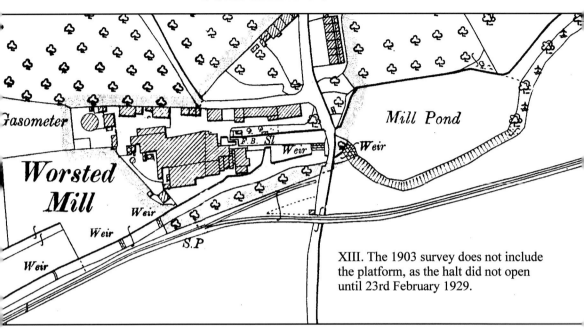

XIII. The 1903 survey does not include the platform, as the halt did not open until 23rd February 1929.

86. The halt was constructed west of the level crossing, backing onto the siding, which could accommodate nine wagons. A notable traffic was coal for the nearby woollen mill.
(Lens of Sutton)

87.　The siding is out of view on the right as no. 1468 proceeds towards Hemyock on 8th July 1959. Goods traffic ceased here when passenger services were withdrawn on 9th September 1963. (R.M.Casserley)

88.　A Hillman 10 and a first generation crossing sign are seen from the south on the same day, together with the two oil lamps. The crossing keeper's accommodation was of GWR design and therefore not original. The site later became part of the mill car park. (R.M.Casserley)

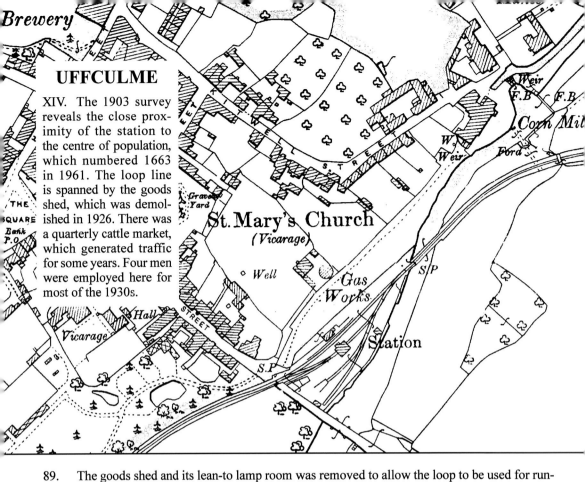

UFFCULME

XIV. The 1903 survey reveals the close proximity of the station to the centre of population, which numbered 1663 in 1961. The loop line is spanned by the goods shed, which was demolished in 1926. There was a quarterly cattle market, which generated traffic for some years. Four men were employed here for most of the 1930s.

89.   The goods shed and its lean-to lamp room was removed to allow the loop to be used for run-round purposes. A mid-morning train from Tiverton Junction terminated here from 1926 to 1963. The cattle trucks (right) delivered livestock to the nearby abattoir, while the insulated vans (in the shed) took away the meat. (G.N.Southernden)

90.   The raised platform and the iron-clad store were provided in 1926 to replace the goods shed. In the background, two grain wagons stand on a siding provided for W.J.Williams in 1919. This was taken over by George Small in about 1935, when the mill was constructed. The siding continued in use after public goods traffic ceased on 6th August 1967. The cattle pen is on the left. (Lens of Sutton)

Uffculme	1903	1913	1923	1933
Passenger tickets issued	8993	7786	6167	7328
Season tickets issued	*	*	80	65
Parcels forwarded	4707	5810	3729	3794
General goods forwarded (tons)	705	1190	1256	335
Coal and coke received (tons)	1451	1395	1135	481
Other minerals received (tons)	333	273	726	467
General goods received (tons)	2265	2308	3762	4551
Trucks of livestock handled	86	217	682	184
(* not available. Seasons include holiday Runabouts.)				

91.   As no. 1451 departs for Hemyock in March 1959, we have the opportunity of seeing the east elevation of the goods shed and that the loop is blocked with coal wagons. The yard length was constrained by the River Culm. The one-ton crane in the goods shed was replaced by one of three-ton capacity in the yard. (H.Cowan)

92.   The bridge over the Culm is on the right of this fine record of no. 1451 with its mixed train on 15th June 1962. This is the 12.10pm departure, the one train to commence its journey here on Mondays to Fridays. The coach is one of two ex-Barry Railway five-compartment gas-lit short coaches that arrived for the branch in 1950; they were scrapped in 1962. (R.C.Riley)

93.   The engineer to the CVLR was Alfred Pain, a light railway pioneer many years prior to the better known Colonel Stephens. He employed this style of building on his lines to Highworth and to Southwold. The gas lights were provided in about 1880; the floral display is seen in 1963. The site is now built over. (C.L.Caddy)

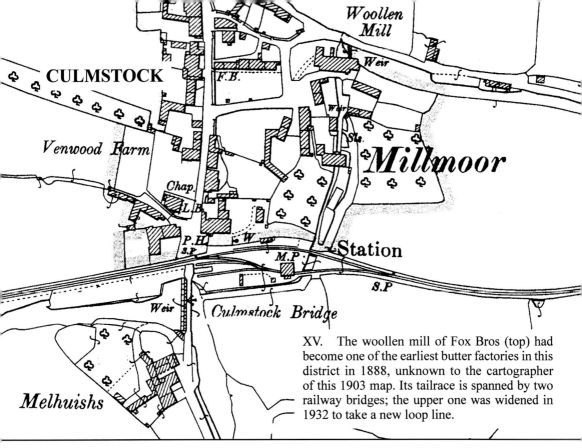

XV.   The woollen mill of Fox Bros (top) had become one of the earliest butter factories in this district in 1888, unknown to the cartographer of this 1903 map. Its tailrace is spanned by two railway bridges; the upper one was widened in 1932 to take a new loop line.

94.   An eastward view reveals that road vehicles had to cross the running line to reach the yard. The tail race from the mill was behind the highest wall on the right. The goods shed was demolished in 1932 to allow the loop to be moved closer to the running line. Two men usually sufficed here. (LGRP/NRM)

95.   An eastward panorama in 1956 includes a train about to depart for Tiverton Junction. The gate to the cattle dock is between the train and Culmstock Bridge. The pole on the left is a reminder of the fact that this station had a telegraph office from 1877. Telephones were provided in 1931. (H.C.Casserley)

96.   No. 1405 is running round the 11.25 from Tiverton Junction on 29th September 1956. The short working to Uffculme was extended here on Saturdays, arriving at 12.0 and departing at 12.7. The ex-Barry coach usually ran solo, except at school times. (H.C.Casserley)

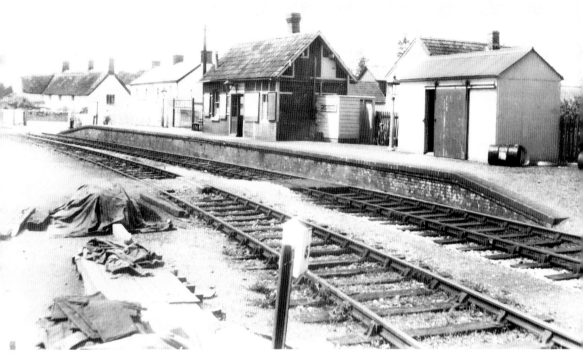

97.   Some of the timber framing *apparent* in picture no. 90 (and also in many views in our *Branch Line to Southwold)* was a sham. Much of it has fallen off in this photograph and others in this volume. The unofficial crossing enabled road vehicles to back up close to the goods shed. (I.D.Beale)

```
   2nd · SINGLE        SINGLE · 2nd
4558          Hemyock to            4558
       Hemyock              Hemyock
       Culmstock            Culmstock

           CULMSTOCK
       (W)    6d   Fare   6d    (W)
       For conditions see over For conditions see over
```

Culmstock	1903	1913	1923	1933
Passenger tickets issued	5608	5375	4403	4511
Season tickets issued	*	*	27	20
Parcels forwarded	2227	2719	2060	2014
General goods forwarded (tons)	196	190	112	52
Coal and coke received (tons)	22	62	46	-
Other minerals received (tons)	157	144	238	97
General goods received (tons)	477	679	667	420
Trucks of livestock handled	82	59	112	120

(* not available. Seasons include holiday Runabouts.)

98.   The station was unstaffed from 2nd May 1960, when it technically became a halt, but the timetables and nameboards were not amended. This 1963 view includes the three oil lamps. The population was about 700 at this time. The goods yard and its 3-ton crane ceased to be used after 7th September 1963. (C.L.Caddy)

99.   Passing the cattle pens on 7th September 1963, the last day of passenger operation, are the line's two exclusive coaches, hauled by no. 1421. The short ex-LNER vehicles had only four compartments each and had usually run singly. They had arrived in 1962 and had to be connected to a battery charger at night, as the 15mph speed limit on the line rendered the generators ineffective. (C.L.Caddy)

100.   The inn in the background had earlier been the Railway Hotel, but there was no sense of history therein it seems. Class 25 no. 7677 is about to pass over the level crossing on 19th February 1973. This type had come to the branch in 1971 following the upgrading of the track. (D.H.Mitchell)

101.   Class 25 no. 7676 returns from Hemyock on 13th October 1973 with loaded milk tankers and extra brake vans carrying members of the RCTS. The platform ramp and cattle dock can be glimpsed, along with the rails in the washing apron. All the buildings on the branch had gone by this time and this site later becme a pub car park. (R.A.Lumber)

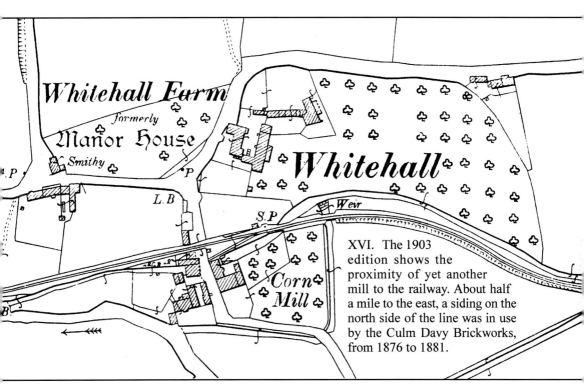

XVI. The 1903 edition shows the proximity of yet another mill to the railway. About half a mile to the east, a siding on the north side of the line was in use by the Culm Davy Brickworks, from 1876 to 1881.

102. The land for the siding was given by a farmer when the line was built, but, despite his pleas, a halt was not provided until 27th February 1933. This 1958 view includes the unusually sited waiting shelter, off the end of the platform. (H.C.Casserley)

103. The crossing keepers hut and the two-lever ground frame are featured. The latter was unlocked with a key attached to the end of the solitary single line train staff. With a "one engine in steam" rule, no signals were needed, although they were demanded (unnecessarily) until 1902. (I.D.Beale)

104.   No. 1421 arrives with the 10.30am from Hemyock on the last day of operation, the siding closing officially on the following Monday. The rod on the right controlled the catch point. The coach is near one of the 31 bridges on the 7½ mile long branch. (C.L.Caddy)

105.   Class 35 no. D7005 waits for the second man to open the gates, as it proceeds to Hemyock on 14th February 1971. This class was rarely used on the branch; classes 08 and 22 were also sometimes seen, but the small 03s were used regularly from 1963. (D.H.Mitchell)

HEMYOCK

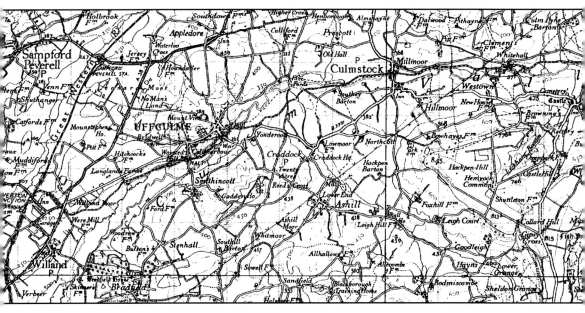

XVII. The 1946 edition at 1ins to 1 mile shows that the terminus was at Millhayes, half a mile north of Hemyock. There was an altitude difference of over 60ft. The severe curvature of the route is evident, this necessitating the provision of short coaches and the banning of push-pull working. Many curves were of only six-chain radius.

XVIII. The 1903 survey includes one line into the mill; a branch northwards from it, within the grounds, was added later. The mill had been taken over by the Culm Valley Dairy Co. in 1886 and this firm became part of United Dairies following its formation in 1915. Butter production ceased here soon after.

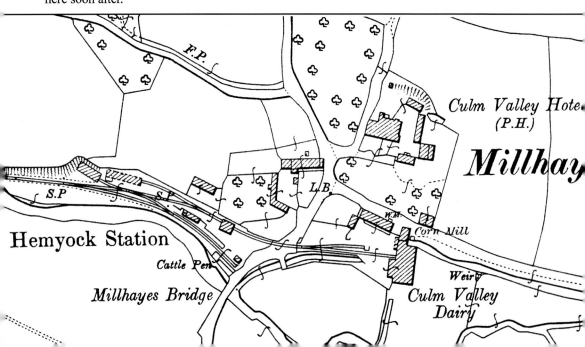

106.   There was an engine shed (left) and a carriage shed (right) until October 1929. Seen in about 1906 is no. 1384, a 2-4-0T built for the Watlington & Princes Risborough Railway in 1876 and sold to the Weston, Clevedon & Portishead Light Railway in 1911. Notice how short the loop was initially. (R.S.Carpenter coll.)

Hemyock	1903	1913	1923	1933
Passenger tickets issued	4237	4341	4242	2286
Season tickets issued	*	*	26	45
Parcels forwarded	15773	19980	30009	9608
General goods forwarded (tons)	428	471	1330	2250
Coal and coke received (tons)	102	95	3165	1487
Other minerals received (tons)	524	514	725	369
General goods received (tons)	2985	3123	3504	3081
Trucks of livestock handled	70	113	148	69

(* not available. Seasons include holiday Runabouts.)

107.   Three photographs follow which feature no. 1300 on 25th May 1929. This locomotive was completed by the GWR in 1878 and worked on the branch between 1881 and 1934. Note that the carriage shed was not boarded to the ground; the same economy was employed on the Talyllyn Railway. (H.C.Casserley)

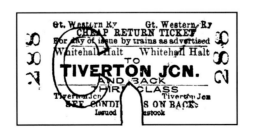

108. The train includes two ex-Manchester & Milford Railway coaches. (The company reached neither place.) The front one would have carried passengers, while the other acted as a brake van. (H.C.Casserley)

109. The coaches were reversed for the return journey, as the wagons did not have continuous brakes. This is the 2.45pm departure, due at Tiverton Junction at 3.31, shunting permitting. (H.C.Casserley)

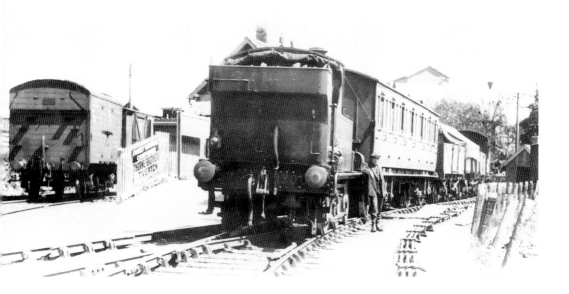

↑ 110. This indifferent picture from about 1930 is included as it shows the goods shed shown on the map. This housed a 30cwt. crane and was demolished at about that time, its replacement being visible in the background of the next picture. (Mowat coll.)

111.	The crane and water tank date from around 1930. The platform had been cut back and the short line on the right provided in 1920. The line on the left was extended over the road to a new factory producing condensed milk on 17th July 1920. The cattle pen is in its original position. (R.C.Riley)

112.	Six-wheeled milk tankers were introduced in 1932 and were fully braked, thus the coach could be attached to the rear of them. No. 1449 is departing on 23rd July 1958. The building behind the leading tanks was erected in 1878 as a refreshment room for the expected crowds of trippers. After one season, it was used to house cattle instead. (R.C.Riley)

113.   The north elevation had a sliding door to facilitate parcel transfer to and from road transport. Much of the "timber framing" is missing, that on the west elevation rotting first. The ugly extension was made with concrete blocks in about 1930 and was used as a waiting room. (Lens of Sutton)

114.   A 1960 view includes tankers in Cow & Gate's Works and the east ground frame, which had seven levers. This was termed a signal box until 1925. Behind it is the gents. Arthur Pain had specified earth closets here (and on the Southwold Railway), but the GWR demanded water closets. The EC was unpopular, but cheaper than a WC. (M.Dart)

115.   The 10.30am departure on 30th September 1961 included a van, but it had to be at the back as it was devoid of continuous brakes. As there was no bracket, the lamp had to go on the coupling hook to indicate a complete train. (J.H.Day)

116.   The level crossing on the left came soon after the line opened, but it did not have gates *across* the road and locomotives were not allowed to use it. The converse applied to the 1920 crossing on the right. The gates in the centre are to the station yard. (S.P.Derek)

117.   No. 1471 is propelling wagons over the original crossing on 19th May 1962, but the engine will stop at the gate. Empty wagons would separate the loco from those to be left at the factory. Loaded tanks would usually be run over the road by gravity, on both sidings. The factory had a winch which could be used to pull wagons over the road while a flagman stopped road users. (S.C.Nash)

118.   The last passenger train ever departs at 6.0pm on Saturday 7th September 1963, hauled by no. 1421, but the goods yard and the 3-ton crane would be available for public traffic until 6th September 1965. The goods shed (left) was subsequently used by a farmer, as was the refreshment room (background), which was on his land already. (R.A.Lumber)

119.   A class 03 0-6-0 diesel first appeared on the branch on 7th September 1963 and this type was used regularly following the demise of steam. No. D2119 was recorded on 29th April 1967. The chock protecting the level crossing is also evident. (M.J.Messenger)

120.   Class 25 no. D7677 arrives with one tanker on 19th February 1973. Note that the loop (left) had been greatly lengthened, compared with picture no. 106. Milk despatched daily rose from 3000 gallons in 1920 to 6000 in 1930, at which period four men were employed at the station. Later six to twelve 3000 gallon tankers would leave here, seven days a week. The creamery closed in October 1975, by which time only fuel oil was conveyed by rail. The branch closed on 1st November 1975, six months short of its centenary. The area became a car park and little evidence remains elsewhere. Thankfully some photographers thoroughly recorded this charming byway for our ongoing pleasure. (D.H.Mitchell)

A
Abergavenny to Merthyr C 91 8
Abertillery & Ebbw Vale Lines D 84 5
Aberystwyth to Carmarthen E 90 1
Alnmouth to Berwick G 50 0
Alton - Branch Lines to A 11 6
Ambergate to Buxton G 28 9
Ambergate to Mansfield G 39 5
Andover to Southampton A 82 6
Ascot - Branch Lines around A 64 2
Ashburton - Branch Line to B 95 4
Ashford - Steam to Eurostar B 67 1
Ashford to Dover A 48 2
Austrian Narrow Gauge D 04 3
Avonmouth - BL around D 42 5
Aylesbury to Rugby D 91 3

B
Baker Street to Uxbridge D 90 6
Bala to Llandudno E 87 1
Banbury to Birmingham D 27 2
Banbury to Cheltenham E 63 5
Bangor to Holyhead F 01 7
Bangor to Portmadoc E 72 7
Barking to Southend C 80 2
Barmouth to Pwllheli E 53 6
Barry - Branch Lines around D 50 0
Bartlow - Branch Lines to F 27 7
Basingstoke to Salisbury A 89 4
Bath Green Park to Bristol C 36 9
Bath to Evercreech Junction A 60 4
Beamish 40 years on rails E94 9
Beattock to Carstairs G 84 5
Bedford to Wellingborough D 31 9
Berwick to Drem F 64 2
Berwick to St. Boswells F 75 8
B'ham to Tamworth & Nuneaton F 63 5
Birkenhead to West Kirby F 61 1
Birmingham to Wolverhampton E253
Blackburn to Hellifield F 95 6
Bletchley to Cambridge D 94 4
Bletchley to Rugby E 07 9
Bodmin - Branch Lines around B 83 1
Bolton to Preston G 61 6
Boston to Lincoln F 80 2
Bournemouth to Evercreech Jn A 46 8
Bradshaw's History F 18 5
Bradshaw's Rail Times 1850 F 13 0
Branch Lines series - see town names
Brecon to Neath D 43 2
Brecon to Newport D 16 6
Brecon to Newtown E 06 2
Brighton to Eastbourne A 16 1
Brighton to Worthing A 03 1
Bristol to Taunton D 03 6
Bromley South to Rochester B 23 7
Bromsgrove to Birmingham D 87 6
Bromsgrove to Gloucester D 73 9
Broxbourne to Cambridge F16 1
Brunel - a railtour D 74 6
Bude - Branch Line to B 29 9
Burnham to Evercreech Jn B 68 0
Buxton to Stockport G 32 6

C
Cambridge to Ely D 55 5
Canterbury - BLs around B 58 9
Cardiff to Dowlais (Cae Harris) E 47 5
Cardiff to Pontypridd E 95 6
Cardiff to Swansea E 42 0
Carlisle to Beattock G 69 2
Carlisle to Hawick E 85 7
Carmarthen to Fishguard E 66 6
Caterham & Tattenham Corner B251
Central & Southern Spain NG E 91 8
Chard and Yeovil - BLs a C 30 7
Charing Cross to Orpington A 96 3
Cheddar - Branch Line to B 90 9
Cheltenham to Andover C 43 7
Cheltenham to Redditch D 81 4
Chesterfield to Lincoln G 21 0
Chester to Birkenhead F 21 5
Chester to Manchester F 51 2
Chester to Rhyl E 93 2
Chester to Warrington F 40 6
Chichester to Portsmouth A 14 7
Clacton and Walton - BLs to F 04 8
Clapham Jn to Beckenham Jn B 36 7
Cleobury Mortimer - BLs a E 18 5
Clevedon & Portishead - BLs to D180

Consett to South Shields E 57 4
Cornwall Narrow Gauge D 56 2
Corris and Vale of Rheidol E 65 9
Coventry to Leicester G 00 5
Craven Arms to Llandeilo E 35 2
Craven Arms to Wellington E 33 8
Crawley to Littlehampton A 34 5
Crewe to Manchester F 57 4
Crewe to Wigan G 12 8
Cromer - Branch Lines around C 26 0
Cromford and High Peak G 35 7
Croydon to East Grinstead B 48 0
Crystal Palace & Catford Loop B 87 1
Cyprus Narrow Gauge E 13 0

D
Darjeeling Revisited F 09 3
Darlington Leamside Newcastle E 28 4
Darlington to Newcastle D 98 2
Dartford to Sittingbourne B 34 3
Denbigh - Branch Lines around F 32 1
Derby to Chesterfield G 11 1
Derby to Nottingham G 45 6
Derby to Stoke-on-Trent F 93 2
Derwent Valley - BL to the D 06 7
Devon Narrow Gauge E 09 3
Didcot to Banbury D 02 9
Didcot to Swindon C 84 0
Didcot to Winchester C 13 0
Diss to Norwich G 22 7
Dorset & Somerset NG D 76 0
Douglas - Laxey - Ramsey E 75 8
Douglas to Peel C 88 8
Douglas to Port Erin C 55 0
Douglas to Ramsey D 39 5
Dover to Ramsgate A 78 9
Drem to Edinburgh G 06 7
Dublin Northwards in 1950s E 31 4
Dunstable - Branch Lines to E 27 7

E
Ealing to Slough C 42 0
Eastbourne to Hastings A 27 7
East Croydon to Three Bridges A 53 6
Eastern Spain Narrow Gauge E 56 7
East Grinstead - BLs to A 07 9
East Kent Light Railway A 61 1
East London - Branch Lines of C 44 4
East London Line B 80 0
East of Norwich - Branch Lines E 69 7
Effingham Junction - BLs a A 74 1
Ely to Norwich C 90 1
Enfield Town & Palace Gates D 32 6
Epsom to Horsham A 30 7
Eritrean Narrow Gauge E 38 3
Euston to Harrow & Wealdstone C 89 5
Exeter to Barnstaple B 15 2
Exeter to Newton Abbot C 49 9
Exeter to Tavistock B 69 9
Exmouth - Branch Lines to B 00 8

F
Fairford - Branch Line to A 52 9
Falmouth, Helston & St. Ives C 74 1
Fareham to Salisbury A 67 3
Faversham to Dover B 05 3
Felixstowe & Aldeburgh - BL to D 20 3
Fenchurch Street to Barking C 20 8
Festiniog - 50 yrs of enterprise C 83 3
Festiniog 1946-55 E 01 7
Festiniog in the Fifties B 68 8
Festiniog in the Sixties B 91 6
Ffestiniog in Colour 1955-82 F 25 3
Finsbury Park to Alexandra Pal C 02 8
French Metre Gauge Survivors F 88 8
Frome to Bristol B 77 0

G
Gainsborough to Sheffield G 17 3
Galashiels to Edinburgh F 52 9
Gloucester to Bristol D 37 7
Gloucester to Cardiff D 66 1
Gosport - Branch Lines around A 36 9
Greece Narrow Gauge D 72 2
Guildford to Redhill A 63 5

H
Hampshire Narrow Gauge D 36 4
Harrow to Watford D 14 2
Harwich & Hadleigh - BLs to F 02 4
Harz Revisited F 62 8
Hastings to Ashford A 37 6
Hawick to Galashiels F 36 9
Hawkhurst - Branch Line to A 66 6

Hayling - Branch Line to A 12 3
Hay-on-Wye - BL around D 92 0
Haywards Heath to Seaford A 28 4
Hemel Hempstead - BLs to D 88 3
Henley, Windsor & Marlow - BLa C77 2
Hereford to Newport D 54 8
Hertford & Hatfield - BLs a E 58 1
Hertford Loop E 71 0
Hexham to Carlisle D 75 3
Hexham to Hawick F 08 6
Hitchin to Peterborough D 07 4
Horsham - Branch Lines to A 02 4
Hull, Hornsea and Withernsea G 27 2
Hull to Scarborough G 60 9
Huntingdon - Branch Line to A 93 2

I
Ilford to Shenfield C 97 0
Ilfracombe - Branch Line to B 21 3
Ilkeston to Chesterfield G 26 5
Inverkeithing to Thornton Jct G 76 0
Ipswich to Diss F 81 9
Ipswich to Saxmundham C 41 3
Isle of Man Railway Journey F 94 9
Isle of Wight Lines - 50 yrs C 12 3
Italy Narrow Gauge F 17 8

K
Kent Narrow Gauge C 45 1
Kettering to Nottingham F 82-6
Kidderminster to Shrewsbury E 10 9
Kingsbridge - Branch Line to C 98 7
Kings Cross to Potters Bar E 62 8
King's Lynn to Hunstanton F 58 1
Kingston & Hounslow Loops A 83 3
Kingswear - Branch Line to C 17 8

L
Lambourn - Branch Line to C 70 3
Lancaster to Oxenholme G 77 7
Launceston & Princetown - BLs C 19 2
Leeds to Selby G 47 0
Leek - Branch Line From G 01 2
Leicester to Burton F 85 7
Leicester to Nottingham G 15 9
Lewisham to Dartford A 92 5
Lincoln to Cleethorpes F 56 7
Lincoln to Doncaster G 03 6
Lines around Newmarket G 54 8
Lines around Stamford F 98 7
Lines around Wimbledon B 75 6
Lines North of Stoke G 29 6
Liverpool to Runcorn G 72 2
Liverpool Street to Chingford D 01 2
Liverpool Street to Ilford C 34 5
Llandeilo to Swansea E 46 8
London Bridge to Addiscombe B 20 6
London Bridge to East Croydon A 58 1
Longmoor - Branch Lines to A 41 3
Looe - Branch Line to C 22 2
Loughborough to Ilkeston G 24 1
Loughborough to Nottingham F 68 0
Lowestoft - BLs around E 40 6
Ludlow to Hereford E 14 7
Lydney - Branch Lines around E 26 0
Lyme Regis - Branch Line to A 45 1
Lynton - Branch Line to B 04 6

M
Machynlleth to Barmouth E 54 3
Maesteg and Tondu Lines F 06 2
Majorca & Corsica Narrow Gauge F 41 3
Manchester to Bacup G 46 3
Mansfield to Doncaster G 23 4
March - Branch Lines around B 09 1
Market Drayton - BLs around F 67 3
Market Harborough to Newark F 86 4
Marylebone to Rickmansworth D 49 4
Melton Constable to Yarmouth Bch E031
Midhurst - Branch Lines of E 78 9
Midhurst - Branch Lines F 00 0
Minehead - Branch Line to A 80 2
Monmouth - Branch Lines to E 20 8
Monmouthshire Eastern Valleys D 71 5
Moretonhampstead - BL to C 27 7
Moreton-in-Marsh to Worcester D 26 5
Morpeth to Bellingham F 87 1
Mountain Ash to Neath D 80 7

N
Newark to Doncaster F 78 9
Newbury to Westbury C 66 6

Newcastle to Alnmouth G 36 4
Newcastle to Hexham D 69 2
Newmarket to Haughley & Laxfield G 71 5
New Mills to Sheffield G 44 9
Newport (IOW) - Branch Lines to A 26 0
Newton Abbot to Plymouth C 60 4
Newtown to Aberystwyth E 41 3
Northampton to Peterborough F 92 5
North East German NG D 44 9
Northern Alpine Narrow Gauge F 37 6
Northern Spain Narrow Gauge E 83 3
North London Line B 94 7
North of Birmingham F 55 0
North of Grimsby - Branch Lines G 09 8
North Woolwich - BLs around C 65 9
Nottingham to Boston F 70 3
Nottingham to Kirkby Bentinck G 38 8
Nottingham to Lincoln F 43 7
Nottingham to Mansfield G 52 4
Nuneaton to Loughborough G 08 1

O
Ongar - Branch Line to E 05 5
Orpington to Tonbridge B 03 8
Oswestry - Branch Lines around E 60 4
Oswestry to Whitchurch E 81 9
Oxford to Bletchley D 57 9
Oxford to Moreton-in-Marsh D 15 9

P
Paddington to Ealing C 37 6
Paddington to Princes Risborough C819
Padstow - Branch Line to D 54 1
Peebles Loop G 19 7
Pembroke and Cardigan - BLs to F 29 1
Peterborough to Kings Lynn E 32 1
Peterborough to Lincoln F 89 5
Peterborough to Newark F 72 7
Plymouth - BLs around B 98 5
Plymouth to St. Austell C 63 5
Pontypool to Mountain Ash D 65 4
Pontypridd to Merthyr F 14 7
Pontypridd to Port Talbot E 86 4
Porthmadog 1954-94 - BLa B 31 2
Portmadoc 1923-46 - BLa B 13 8
Portsmouth to Southampton A 31 4
Portugal Narrow Gauge E 67 3
Potters Bar to Cambridge D 70 8
Preston to Blackpool G 16 6
Preston to the Fylde Coast G 81 4
Preston to Lancaster G 74 6
Princes Risborough - BL to D 05 0
Princes Risborough to Banbury C 85 7

R
Railways to Victory C 16 1
Reading to Basingstoke B 27 5
Reading to Didcot C 79 6
Reading to Guildford A 47 5
Redhill to Ashford A 73 4
Return to Blaenau 1970-82 C 64 2
Rhyl to Bangor F 15 4
Rhymney & New Tredegar Lines E 48 2
Rickmansworth to Aylesbury D 61 6
Romania & Bulgaria NG E 23 9
Ross-on-Wye - BLs around E 30 7
Ruabon to Barmouth E 84 0
Rugby to Birmingham E 37 6
Rugby to Loughborough F 12 3
Rugby to Stafford F 07 9
Rugeley to Stoke-on-Trent F 90 1
Ryde to Ventnor A 19 2

S
Salisbury to Westbury B 39 8
Salisbury to Yeovil B 06 0
Sardinia and Sicily Narrow Gauge F 50 5
Saxmundham to Yarmouth C 69 7
Saxony & Baltic Germany Revisited F 71 0
Saxony Narrow Gauge D 47 0
Scunthorpe to Doncaster G 34 0
Seaton & Sidmouth - BLs to A 95 6
Selsey - Branch Line to A 04 8
Sheerness - Branch Line to B 16 2
Sheffield towards Manchester G 18 0
Shenfield to Ipswich E 96 3
Shildon to Stockton G 79 1
Shrewsbury - Branch Line to A 86 4
Shrewsbury to Chester E 70 3
Shrewsbury to Crewe F 48 2
Shrewsbury to Ludlow E 21 5
Shrewsbury to Newtown E 29 1
Sirhowy Valley Line E 12 3
Sittingbourne to Ramsgate A 90 1
Skegness & Mablethorpe - BL to F 84 0
Slough to Newbury C 56 7
South African Two-foot gauge E 51 2
Southampton to Bournemouth A 42 0
Southend & Southminster BLs E 76 5
Southern Alpine Narrow Gauge F 22 2

South London Line B 46 6
South Lynn to Norwich City F 03 1
Southwold - Branch Line to A 15 4
Spalding - Branch Lines around E 52 9
Spalding to Grimsby F 65 9 6
Stafford to Chester F 34 5
Stafford to Wellington F 59 8
St Albans to Bedford D 08 1
St. Austell to Penzance C 67 3
St. Boswell to Berwick F 44 4
Stourbridge to Wolverhampton E 16 9
St. Pancras to Barking D 68 5
St. Pancras to Folkestone E 88 8
St. Pancras to St. Albans C 78 9
Stratford to Cheshunt F 53 6
Stratford-u-Avon to Birmingham D 77 0
Stratford-u-Avon to Cheltenham C 25 8
Sudbury - Branch Lines to F 19 2
Surrey Narrow Gauge C 87 1
Sussex Narrow Gauge C 68 0
Swaffham - Branch Lines around F 93 9
Swanage to 1999 - BL to A 33 8
Swanley to Ashford B 45 9
Swansea - Branch Lines around F 38 3
Swansea to Carmarthen E 59 8
Swindon to Bristol C 96 3
Swindon to Gloucester D 46 3
Swindon to Newport D 30 2
Swiss Narrow Gauge C 94 9

T
Talyllyn 60 E 98 7
Tamworth to Derby F 76 5
Taunton to Barnstaple B 64 2
Taunton to Exeter C 82 6
Taunton to Minehead F 39 0
Tavistock to Plymouth B 88 6
Tenterden - Branch Line to A 21 5
Three Bridges to Brighton A 35 2
Tilbury Loop C 86 4
Tiverton - BLs around C 62 8
Tivetshall to Beccles D 41 8
Tonbridge to Hastings A 44 4
Torrington - Branch Lines to B 37 4
Tourist Railways of France G 04 3
Towcester - BLs around E 39 0
Tunbridge Wells BLs A 32 1

U
Upwell - Branch Line to B 64 0
Uttoxeter to Macclesfield G 05 0
Uttoxeter to Buxton G 33 3

V
Victoria to Bromley South A 98 7
Victoria to East Croydon A 40 6
Vivarais Revisited E 08 6

W
Walsall Routes F 45 1
Wantage - Branch Line to D 25 8
Wareham to Swanage 50 yrs D 09 8
Watercress Line G 75 3
Waterloo to Windsor A 54 3
Waterloo to Woking A 38 3
Watford to Leighton Buzzard D 45 9
Wellingborough to Leicester F 73 4
Welshpool to Llanfair E 49 9
Wenford Bridge to Fowey C 09 3
Wennington to Morecambe G 58 6
Westbury to Bath B 55 8
Westbury to Taunton C 76 5
West Cornwall Mineral Rlys D 14 7
West Croydon to Epsom B 08 4
West German Narrow Gauge D 93 7
West London - BLs of C 50 0
West London Line B 84 8
West Somerset Railway G 78 4
West Wiltshire - BLs of D 12 8
Weymouth - BLs A 65 9
Willesden Jn to Richmond B 71 8
Wimbledon to Beckenham C 58 1
Wimbledon to Epsom B 62 6
Wimborne - BLs around A 97 0
Wirksworth - Branch Lines to G 10 4
Wisbech - BLs around C 01 7
Witham & Kelvedon - BLs a E 82 6
Woking to Alton A 59 8
Woking to Portsmouth A 25 3
Woking to Southampton A 55 0
Wolverhampton to Shrewsbury E 44 0
Wolverhampton to Stafford F 79 6
Worcester to Birmingham D 97 5
Worcester to Hereford D 38 8
Worthing to Chichester A 06 2
Wrexham to New Brighton F 47 5
Wroxham - BLs around F 31 4

Y
Yeovil - 50 yrs change C 38 3
Yeovil to Dorchester A 76 5
Yeovil to Exeter A 91 8
York to Scarborough F 23 9